GREEN
EATING

Publications International, Ltd.

Pictured on the front cover: Pesto Zoodles with Potatoes *(page 174).*

Pictured on the back cover *(left to right, top to bottom):* Warm Goat Cheese Salad *(page 42)*, French Lentil Rice Soup *(page 150)*, Beet Noodles with Edamame, Spinach and Feta *(page 132)*, Cold Peanut Noodle and Edamame Salad *(page 70) and* Pear Ginger Juice *(page 184).*

ISBN: 978-1-68022-760-4

Library of Congress Control Number: 2016954069

Manufactured in China.

8 7 6 5 4 3 2 1

Publications International, Ltd.

CONTENTS

INTRODUCTION

TIPS FOR GREEN EATING

• Base your meals around whole, minimally-processed foods: whole grains, fresh produce (local whenever possible), nuts and dried legumes, and avoid highly processed foods along with trans fats and high fructose corn syrup.

• Eat the rainbow for nutritional benefits.

• Eat your leftovers and avoid food waste. Don't buy more than you know you'll use and plan meals that can become something new the next night (leftover rice and beans becomes tacos, leftover soup becomes a sauce for pasta).

• Use up extra produce in juices and smoothies (pages 176–188). Blending and juicing are forgiving and can be a great way to use up leftover bits of produce that may otherwise go to waste.

• Limit animal products because of the toll that their production takes on the environment. When you do choose to eat meat or fish, purchase it from producers that use sustainable farming practices.

TIPS FOR GREEN LIVING

• Bring your own bags to the grocery store and skip plastic produce bags whenever possible. (Don't worry— your apples and onions will be fine!)

• Bring your lunch. Many of the recipes in this book make easy, packable lunches. Pack leftovers into reusable containers or make one salad, noodle dish or soup that you'll eat throughout the week. Soups, stews and grain and noodle dishes will keep for a few days in jars in your refrigerator, so make a double batch for dinner and have enough leftover for lunches. Pack salads and dressings in separate containers and mix them together just before eating.

• Take advantage of bulk bins for grains, seeds, nuts and dried beans. You'll get more for less and cut down on packaging waste.

• Shop farmers' markets and look for produce labeled "local" at your grocery store.

• Plant an herb garden in your kitchen or yard with the herbs that you use most.

PANTRY STAPLES

A number of recipes in this book rely on vegetable broth and beans. Resist the temptation to use packaged broth and canned beans—they're convenient but making your own broth and using dried beans are greener options. Broth is easy to make and will use up any odds and ends left in your fridge or pantry: half onions, soft celery, wilted carrots, leftover herbs and even sun-dried tomatoes will make a broth that beats the packaged stuff any day.

HOMEMADE VEGETABLE BROTH

This recipe is just a guideline; broth is very flexible and can accommodate as much or as little as you want to put in it.

- 1 tablespoon olive oil
- 1 to 2 onions (with papery skin), cut into wedges
- 1 to 2 stalks celery (untrimmed), cut into large pieces
- 2 carrots, cut into large pieces
- 2 to 3 unpeeled cloves garlic, crushed
- 8 to 12 cups water
- 1 bunch fresh parsley
   Fresh herb sprigs or dried herbs
- 1 tablespoon whole peppercorns or ½ teaspoon coarsely ground black pepper
- 1 tablespoon salt

Heat oil in stockpot over high heat. Add onion, celery, carrots and garlic; cook 5 minutes, stirring occasionally. Add water, parsley, herbs, salt and pepper. Cover and bring to a boil.

Reduce heat to medium-low; simmer, covered, 30 minutes to 1 hour. Strain solids. Use immediately or store in tightly sealed jars in the refrigerator up to a week.

Makes 8 to 12 cups

COOKING DRIED BEANS

Canned beans are convenient, but you'll save money, reduce packaging waste and arguably have tastier beans if you start from dried.

It takes a bit of advance preparation to use dried beans, but plan on using them a few times in a week and make a big batch one day to use for several meals. You can cook several kinds of beans together, just make sure they're of a similar size so they'll cook at about the same rate. You can also substitute pretty much any kind of bean for another in a recipe depending on what you have on hand.

To substitute dried beans for canned in a recipe, plan on ¾ cup dried beans for every 15-ounce can. A can is about 1½ cups drained (2 cups with liquid), and dried beans will at least double in volume when cooked.

To prepare dried beans, rinse them under cold running water and pick out any debris or blemished beans. For overnight soaking, place them in a large saucepan or bowl and cover with 3 inches of water. Cover and let stand at least 6 hours or overnight.

For quick soaking, place the beans in a large saucepan and cover with 3 inches of water. Bring to a boil over high heat and boil for 2 minutes. Remove the pan from the heat and let stand, covered, for 1 to 2 hours.

To finish cooking the beans for both methods, drain, rinse and return them to the saucepan. Add fresh water to cover by 3 inches. Cover and bring to a boil over high heat. Reduce the heat to medium-low and simmer, uncovered, about 30 minutes or until desired tenderness is reached. Don't add salt or anything acidic (lemon juice, tomatoes, etc.) until the very end of cooking.

BREAKFAST

RAISIN-NUT OATMEAL

- 2¾ cups water
- 1 cup milk
- 2⅔ cups old-fashioned oats
- ⅔ cup raisins
- ½ cup sliced almonds, toasted*
- ⅓ cup packed brown sugar
- ½ teaspoon salt
- ½ teaspoon ground cinnamon
- ⅛ teaspoon ground ginger

To toast nuts, place in nonstick skillet. Cook and stir 5 minutes over medium-low heat or until nuts begin to brown. Spread on plate to cool.

1. Bring water and milk to a boil in large saucepan over high heat. Stir in oats, raisins, almonds, brown sugar, salt, cinnamon and ginger.

2. Reduce heat to medium. Cook and stir 4 to 5 minutes or until thick and creamy.

ZUCCHINI BREAD PANCAKES

1 medium zucchini, grated

¼ cup plain yogurt

1 egg

2 tablespoons milk

1 tablespoon vegetable oil

½ cup whole wheat flour

2 tablespoons packed brown sugar

1 teaspoon grated lemon peel, plus additional for garnish

1 teaspoon baking soda

½ teaspoon ground cinnamon

½ teaspoon vanilla

⅛ teaspoon ground nutmeg

Maple syrup (optional)

1. Combine zucchini, yogurt, egg, milk and oil in large bowl; mix well. Add flour, brown sugar, 1 teaspoon lemon peel, baking soda, cinnamon, vanilla and nutmeg; stir just until combined.

2. Heat nonstick griddle or large nonstick skillet over medium-low heat. Pour ¼ cupfuls of batter 2 inches apart onto griddle. Cook 3 minutes or until lightly browned and edges begin to bubble. Turn over; cook 3 minutes or until lightly browned. Repeat with remaining batter.

3. Serve with maple syrup, if desired. Garnish with additional lemon peel.

MAPLE PECAN GRANOLA

Makes about 6 cups

¼ cup maple syrup

¼ cup packed dark brown sugar

1½ teaspoons vanilla

½ teaspoon ground cinnamon

½ teaspoon coarse salt

6 tablespoons vegetable oil

3 cups old-fashioned oats

¼ cup ground flaxseed

¾ cup shredded coconut

1½ cups pecans, coarsely chopped

¼ cup water

Plain yogurt or milk (optional)

1. Preheat oven to 350°F. Line large rimmed baking sheet with parchment paper.

2. Whisk maple syrup, brown sugar, vanilla, cinnamon, salt and oil in large bowl. Stir in oats, flaxseed, coconut and pecans until evenly coated. Stir in water. Spread mixture evenly on prepared baking sheet, pressing into even layer.

3. Bake 30 minutes or until mixture is golden brown and fragrant. Cool completely on baking sheet. Serve with yogurt or milk, if desired. Store leftovers in an airtight container at room temperature 1 month.

Note: For chunky granola, do not stir during baking. For loose granola, stir every 10 minutes during baking.

SUPER OATMEAL

Makes 4 to 6 servings

2 cups water

2¾ cups old-fashioned oats

½ cup finely diced dried figs

⅓ cup packed dark brown sugar

⅓ to ½ cup sliced almonds, toasted*

¼ cup flaxseeds

½ teaspoon salt

½ teaspoon ground cinnamon

2 cups milk, plus additional for serving

*To toast nuts, place in nonstick skillet. Cook and stir 5 minutes over medium-low heat or until nuts begin to brown. Spread on plate to cool.

1. Bring water to a boil over high heat in large saucepan. Stir in oats, figs, brown sugar, almonds, flaxseeds, salt and cinnamon. Stir in 2 cups milk.

2. Reduce heat to medium-high. Cook and stir 5 to 7 minutes or until oatmeal is thick and creamy. Spoon into serving bowls. Serve with additional milk, if desired.

PUMPKIN GRANOLA

Makes about 5½ cups

3 cups old-fashioned oats

¾ cup coarsely chopped almonds

¾ cup raw pumpkin seeds (pepitas)

½ cup canned pumpkin

½ cup maple syrup

⅓ cup coconut oil, melted

1 teaspoon vanilla

1 teaspoon ground cinnamon

½ teaspoon salt

¼ teaspoon ground ginger

¼ teaspoon ground nutmeg

Pinch ground cloves

¾ cup dried cranberries

1. Preheat oven to 325°F. Line large rimmed baking sheet with parchment paper.

2. Combine oats, almonds and pumpkin seeds in large bowl. Combine pumpkin, maple syrup, oil, vanilla, cinnamon, salt, ginger, nutmeg and cloves in medium bowl; stir until well blended. Pour over oat mixture; stir until well blended and ingredients are completely coated. Spread mixture evenly on prepared baking sheet.

3. Bake 50 to 60 minutes or until granola is golden brown and no longer moist, stirring every 20 minutes. (Granola will become more crisp as it cools.) Stir in cranberries; cool completely.

Pumpkin Chocolate Granola: Follow recipe above but reduce amount of maple syrup to ⅓ cup. Stir in ¾ cup semisweet chocolate chips after baking. You can substitute pecans or walnuts for the almonds, and/or add ¾ cup flaked coconut to the mixture before baking.

SPICED STEEL OAT GRIDDLE CAKES

Makes 6 servings

⅔ cup whole wheat flour

¼ cup steel-cut oats

1 tablespoon baking powder

½ teaspoon ground cinnamon

¼ teaspoon ground nutmeg

¼ teaspoon ground ginger

¼ teaspoon salt

1 cup milk

2 eggs

1 tablespoon vegetable oil

2 teaspoons honey

¼ cup chopped walnuts, plus additional for serving

Maple syrup or honey

1. Combine flour, oats, baking powder, cinnamon, nutmeg, ginger and salt in medium bowl; mix well. Whisk milk, eggs, oil and honey in large bowl until smooth and well blended. Stir into flour mixture until smooth. Let stand 15 minutes. Stir in ¼ cup walnuts.

2. Heat nonstick griddle or large nonstick skillet over medium-low heat. Spoon 2 tablespoons batter 1 inch apart onto griddle. Cook 2 minutes or until bubbles begin to form on top. Turn over; cook 1 minute. Remove to plate and keep warm. Repeat with remaining batter. Serve with maple syrup and additional walnuts, if desired.

WARM APPLE AND BLUEBERRY CRISP

Makes 6 servings

6 apples, peeled and sliced

2 cups frozen blueberries

½ cup packed brown sugar, divided

¼ cup orange juice

½ cup all-purpose flour

½ cup old-fashioned oats

¼ cup (½ stick) cold butter, cut into small pieces

¼ teaspoon ground cinnamon

¼ teaspoon ground ginger

1. Preheat oven to 375°F. Spray 9-inch square baking pan with nonstick cooking spray.

2. Combine apples, blueberries, ¼ cup brown sugar and orange juice in medium bowl; toss to coat. Spoon into prepared pan.

3. Combine flour, oats, remaining ¼ cup brown sugar, butter, cinnamon and ginger in small bowl; mix with fingertips until coarse crumbs form. Sprinkle over fruit mixture.

4. Bake 45 minutes or until apples are tender and topping is golden brown.

SUNNY SEED
BRAN WAFFLES

Makes 4 servings

2 eggs, separated

1 tablespoon packed dark brown sugar

1 tablespoon canola or vegetable oil

1 cup milk

⅔ cup unprocessed wheat bran

⅔ cup quick oats

1½ teaspoons baking powder

¼ teaspoon salt

3 tablespoons sunflower seeds, toasted*

1 cup apple butter

*To toast sunflower seeds, cook and stir in small nonstick skillet over medium heat about 5 minutes or until golden brown. Remove from skillet; let cool.

1. Beat egg whites in medium bowl with electric mixer until soft peaks form. Whisk egg yolks, brown sugar and oil in small bowl. Stir in milk; mix well.

2. Combine bran, oats, baking powder and salt in large bowl; mix well. Stir in milk mixture. Add sunflower seeds; stir just until moistened. Do not overmix. Gently fold in beaten egg whites.

3. Lightly grease waffle iron; heat according to manufacturer's directions. Stir batter; spoon ½ cup batter into waffle iron for each waffle. Cook until steam stops escaping from around edges and waffle is golden brown. Serve with apple butter.

POTATO-ZUCCHINI PANCAKES WITH WARM CORN SALSA

Makes 6 servings

Warm Corn Salsa
(recipe follows)

2 cups frozen hash brown potatoes, thawed and squeezed dry

1½ cups shredded zucchini, squeezed dry

2 eggs

¼ cup all-purpose flour

2 tablespoons chopped onion

2 tablespoons chopped green bell pepper

¼ teaspoon salt

⅛ teaspoon black pepper

1. Prepare Warm Corn Salsa; keep warm.

2. Combine potatoes, zucchini, eggs, flour, onion, bell pepper, salt and black pepper in medium bowl; gently mix.

3. Spray large skillet with nonstick cooking spray; heat over medium-high heat. Working in batches, drop ¼ cupfuls potato mixture into skillet. Cook 3 minutes per side or until golden brown.

4. Serve with salsa.

WARM CORN SALSA

Makes 3 cups

1 tablespoon olive oil

2 tablespoons chopped onion

2 tablespoons finely chopped green bell pepper

2 cups corn kernels

1 cup chunky salsa

2 teaspoons chopped fresh cilantro

Heat oil in medium skillet. Add onion and bell pepper; cook and stir 3 minutes or until crisp-tender. Add corn, salsa and cilantro. Reduce heat to medium-low. Cook 5 minutes or until heated through.

BUCKWHEAT PANCAKES

1 cup buckwheat flour

2 tablespoons cornstarch

2 teaspoons baking powder

¼ teaspoon salt

¼ teaspoon ground cinnamon

1 cup whole milk

1 egg

2 tablespoons butter, melted, plus additional for cooking

2 tablespoons maple syrup, plus additional for serving

½ teaspoon vanilla

1. Whisk flour, cornstarch, baking powder, salt and cinnamon in medium bowl. Whisk milk, egg, 2 tablespoons butter, 2 tablespoons maple syrup and vanilla in small bowl. Gradually whisk into dry ingredients just until combined. Let stand 5 minutes. (Batter will be thick and elastic.)

2. Brush additional butter on griddle or large nonstick skillet; heat over medium heat. Pour ¼ cupfuls of batter 2 inches apart onto griddle. Cook 2 minutes or until lightly browned and edges begin to bubble. Turn over; cook 2 minutes or until lightly browned. Serve with additional maple syrup.

Variation: Add ½ cup blueberries to the batter.

CHERRY OATMEAL

3 cups water

1 cup milk, plus additional for serving

3 cups old-fashioned oats

½ cup dried cherries

⅓ cup packed dark brown sugar

½ teaspoon salt

1. Bring water and 1 cup milk to a boil in large saucepan over high heat. Stir in oats, cherries, brown sugar and salt.

2. Reduce heat to medium-high. Cook and stir 4 to 5 minutes or until thick and creamy. Serve with additional milk, if desired.

GREEN SALADS

CORN, AVOCADO AND RED ONION SALAD

Makes 4 servings

1 cup cooked fresh or thawed frozen corn

1 avocado, diced

1 small green bell pepper

½ red onion, thinly sliced

1 tablespoon white wine vinegar

¼ teaspoon salt

⅛ teaspoon black pepper

Pinch ground cumin

3 tablespoons olive oil

4 cups mixed salad greens or chopped romaine lettuce

1. Combine corn, avocado, bell pepper and onion in large bowl.

2. Combine vinegar, salt, black pepper and cumin in small bowl; stir until salt is dissolved. Whisk in oil. Pour over vegetables; mix well. Serve on greens.

SPRING GREENS WITH BLUEBERRIES, WALNUTS AND FETA

Makes 4 servings

1 tablespoon canola oil

1 tablespoon white wine vinegar or sherry vinegar

2 teaspoons Dijon mustard

½ teaspoon salt

½ teaspoon black pepper

5 cups mixed spring greens (5 ounces)

1 cup fresh blueberries

½ cup crumbled feta cheese

¼ cup chopped walnuts or pecans, toasted*

To toast nuts, place in nonstick skillet. Cook and stir 5 minutes over medium-low heat or until nuts begin to brown. Spread on plate to cool.

1. For dressing, whisk oil, vinegar, mustard, salt, and pepper in large bowl.

2. Add greens and blueberries; toss gently to coat. Top with cheese and walnuts. Serve immediately.

MAIN-DISH MEDITERRANEAN SALAD

Makes 4 servings

8 ounces fresh green beans, ends trimmed

¼ cup olive oil

¼ cup cider vinegar or white vinegar

1 tablespoon Dijon mustard

½ teaspoon salt

¼ teaspoon black pepper

1 package (10 ounces) romaine lettuce, chopped

1 can or pouch (5 ounces) solid white tuna, flaked

8 ounces cherry tomatoes, halved

1. Bring large saucepan of water to a boil. Add green beans; cook 4 minutes or until crisp-tender. Drain and rinse under cold water to stop cooking.

2. Meanwhile for dressing, whisk oil, vinegar, mustard, salt and pepper in small bowl until blended.

3. Combine lettuce, green beans, tuna and tomatoes in large bowl. Drizzle dressing over salad; toss to coat.

MIXED GREENS WITH PEAR AND GOAT CHEESE

Makes 4 servings

¼ cup balsamic vinegar

2 tablespoons olive oil

2 tablespoons honey

1 clove garlic, minced

½ teaspoon salt

¼ teaspoon black pepper

6 cups (about 5 ounces) mixed spring greens

2 pears, thinly sliced

1 cup chopped cooked chicken (about 5 ounces)

½ cup chopped celery

⅓ cup crumbled goat cheese

2 tablespoons slivered almonds

1. For dressing, whisk vinegar, oil, honey, garlic, salt and pepper in small bowl until well blended.

2. Combine greens, pears, chicken, celery and goat cheese in large bowl. Drizzle dressing over salad; toss gently to coat. Top with almonds.

ITALIAN BREAD SALAD

Makes 4 servings

3 slices (½-inch-thick) day-old whole wheat bread

½ cup buttermilk

1 small clove garlic, minced

1 tablespoon minced fresh dill *or* 1 teaspoon dried dill weed

1½ teaspoons onion powder

¼ teaspoon black pepper

2 large tomatoes, cored and cut into 1-inch cubes

1 small cucumber, peeled, cut lengthwise into halves, seeded and thinly sliced

1 small stalk celery, thinly sliced

2 tablespoons minced fresh parsley

⅛ teaspoon salt

1. Preheat oven to 400°F. Cut bread into 1-inch pieces; place on baking sheet. Bake 5 to 7 minutes or until lightly toasted and dry, stirring occasionally. Let cool.

2. For dressing, combine buttermilk, garlic, dill, onion powder and pepper in small jar with tight-fitting lid; shake well. Let stand 15 minutes to allow flavors to blend.

3. Combine tomatoes, cucumber, celery and parsley in large bowl. Sprinkle with salt; toss well.

4. Just before serving, toss toasted bread with vegetables. Shake dressing; pour over salad and toss to coat. Serve immediately.

WARM GOAT CHEESE SALAD

Makes 4 servings

2 tablespoons cornstarch

1 egg white, lightly beaten

½ cup sliced almonds

1 log (4 ounces) goat cheese, chilled

¼ cup sun-dried tomatoes (not packed in oil)

¼ cup plus 2 tablespoons olive oil, divided

2 tablespoons balsamic vinegar

¼ teaspoon salt

¼ teaspoon black pepper

6 cups mixed baby greens (12 ounces)

1 cup seedless red grapes, halved

1. Place cornstarch in shallow dish. Place egg white in another shallow dish. Place almonds in third shallow dish.

2. Cut goat cheese into 8 equal slices using thin knife dipped in hot water. Working with one slice at a time, coat goat cheese with cornstarch; shake off excess. Dip in egg, letting excess drip back into dish. Coat with almonds, pressing lightly to adhere. Place on small plate. Repeat with remaining slices. Refrigerate 15 minutes or until firm.

3. Meanwhile, combine sun-dried tomatoes, ¼ cup oil, vinegar, salt and pepper in blender or food processor; blend until smooth.

4. Heat remaining 2 tablespoons oil in medium nonstick skillet over medium heat. Add goat cheese slices; cook 2 to 3 minutes per side or until golden brown. Remove using slotted spoon to paper towel-lined plate.

5. Divide baby greens and grapes evenly among four plates. Top with goat cheese slices. Drizzle with dressing. Serve immediately.

MEDITERRANEAN CHICKEN SALAD

Makes 2 servings

1 cup Garlic Croutons
  (recipe follows)

¼ cup olive oil

2 tablespoons white
  wine vinegar

1 teaspoon minced
  garlic

1 teaspoon Dijon
  mustard

½ teaspoon salt

½ teaspoon sugar

½ teaspoon dried basil
  or oregano

¼ teaspoon black
  pepper

5 cups spring salad
  greens or mesclun

1 cup diced or
  shredded cooked
  chicken breast

2 plum tomatoes,
  sliced

¼ cup chopped fresh
  basil

1. Prepare Garlic Croutons.

2. For dressing, whisk oil, vinegar, garlic, mustard, salt, sugar, dried basil and black pepper in small bowl until well blended.

3. Combine greens, chicken, tomatoes, fresh basil and 1 cup croutons in large bowl. Add dressing; toss to coat.

GARLIC CROUTONS

Makes 2 cups

5 slices firm white bread

2 tablespoons olive oil

1 clove garlic, minced

¼ teaspoon paprika

1. Preheat oven to 300°F. Trim crusts from bread; cut into ½-inch cubes.

2. Heat oil in skillet over medium heat. Stir in garlic and paprika. Add bread; cook and stir 1 minute just until bread is evenly coated with oil.

3. Spread bread on baking sheet. Bake 20 to 25 minutes until crisp and golden. Let cool.

ASIAN TOFU SALAD

½ (14-ounce) package extra-firm tofu, drained

¼ cup rice vinegar

3 tablespoons reduced-sodium soy sauce

1½ tablespoons sugar

1 tablespoon dark sesame oil

1 to 2 teaspoons chili garlic sauce

1 teaspoon grated ginger

1 cup snow peas, trimmed

8 cups mixed salad greens

2 medium carrots, julienned

1 medium cucumber, thinly sliced

¼ cup dry roasted peanuts, coarsely chopped

1. Cut tofu into ½-inch cubes; place in single layer on clean kitchen towel.

2. Whisk vinegar, soy sauce, sugar, sesame oil, chili garlic sauce and ginger in small bowl.

3. Heat nonstick skillet over medium-high heat; add tofu, 2 tablespoons sauce mixture and snow peas. Cook and stir 5 to 7 minutes. Let cool slightly.

4. Combine mixed greens, carrots and cucumber in large bowl. Drizzle with remaining sauce mixture and toss to mix.

5. Add warm tofu mixture and peanuts. Serve immediately.

GREENS WITH CRANBERRIES AND BALSAMIC VINAIGRETTE

Makes 4 servings

½ cup pecan halves

¼ cup vegetable oil

2 tablespoons soy sauce

2 to 3 tablespoons balsamic vinegar

2 tablespoons packed dark brown sugar

1 teaspoon grated fresh ginger

½ teaspoon red pepper flakes

5 cups (5 ounces) mixed spring greens

½ cup dried cranberries

½ cup thinly sliced red onion

½ cup crumbled blue cheese or goat cheese

1. Heat medium skillet over medium-high heat. Add pecans and cook 2 to 3 minutes or until just beginning to lightly brown, stirring constantly. Set aside to cool.

2. For dressing, whisk oil, soy sauce, vinegar, brown sugar, ginger and red pepper flakes in small bowl.

3. Combine greens, cranberries and onion in large bowl. Add dressing; toss to coat. Top with pecans and cheese.

ZESTY ZUCCHINI CHICKPEA SALAD

Makes 4 to 6 servings

3 medium zucchini

½ teaspoon salt

5 tablespoons white vinegar

1 clove garlic, minced

¼ teaspoon dried thyme

½ cup olive oil

1 cup canned chickpeas, rinsed and drained

½ cup sliced pitted black olives

3 green onions, minced

1 canned chipotle pepper in adobo sauce, drained, seeded and minced

1 ripe avocado

⅓ cup crumbled feta cheese

Bibb lettuce leaves

Sliced tomato (optional)

1. Cut zucchini lengthwise into halves; cut halves crosswise into ¼-inch-thick slices. Place in medium bowl; sprinkle with salt. Toss to mix. Place in colander in sink; let stand 30 minutes to drain.

2. Combine vinegar, garlic and thyme in large bowl. Gradually whisk in oil until dressing is thoroughly blended. Pat zucchini dry; add to dressing. Add chickpeas, olives and green onions; toss lightly to coat. Cover; refrigerate at least 30 minutes or up to 4 hours, stirring occasionally.

3. Just before serving, stir in chipotle pepper. Cut avocado into ½-inch cubes. Add avocado and cheese to salad; toss lightly to mix. Serve salad in lettuce-lined bowl. Garnish with tomato, if desired.

GREENS AND PEAR WITH MAPLE-MUSTARD DRESSING

Makes 4 servings

- ¼ cup maple syrup
- 1 tablespoon Dijon mustard
- 1 tablespoon olive oil
- 1 tablespoon balsamic or cider vinegar
- ⅛ teaspoon salt
- ⅛ teaspoon black pepper
- 4 cups torn mixed salad greens
- 1 medium red pear, cored and thinly sliced
- ¼ cup sliced green onions
- ¼ cup dried cherries
- ¼ cup chopped walnuts, toasted*

To toast nuts, place in nonstick skillet. Cook and stir 5 minutes over medium-low heat or until nuts begin to brown. Spread on plate to cool.

1. For dressing, whisk maple syrup, mustard, oil, vinegar, salt and pepper in small bowl until well blended.

2. Combine greens, pear, green onions, cherries and walnuts in large serving bowl. Drizzle with dressing; gently toss to coat.

STRAWBERRY SPINACH SALAD WITH POPPY SEED DRESSING

¼ cup canola oil

¼ cup unseasoned rice vinegar or raspberry vinegar

4 teaspoons honey

2 teaspoons ground dry mustard

1 teaspoon poppy seeds

¼ teaspoon salt

⅛ teaspoon black pepper

6 cups baby spinach

8 fresh strawberries, stemmed and halved

½ cup pecans, chopped and toasted

¼ cup sliced red onion

2 ounces goat cheese, crumbled

To toast nuts, place in nonstick skillet. Cook and stir 5 minutes over medium-low heat or until nuts begin to brown. Spread on plate to cool.

1. For dressing, whisk oil, vinegar, honey, mustard, poppy seeds, salt and pepper in small bowl until well blended.

2. Divide spinach among four plates. Top with strawberries, pecans, onion and cheese. Drizzle with dressing.

TOMATO, AVOCADO AND CUCUMBER SALAD WITH FETA

Makes 4 servings

2 tablespoons extra virgin olive oil

2 tablespoons balsamic vinegar

1 clove garlic, minced

¼ teaspoon salt

¼ teaspoon black pepper

2 cups diced seeded plum tomatoes

1 small ripe avocado, cut into ½-inch cubes

½ cup chopped cucumber

⅓ cup crumbled feta cheese

4 large red leaf lettuce leaves

Chopped fresh basil (optional)

1. Whisk oil, vinegar, garlic, salt and pepper in medium bowl. Add tomatoes and avocado; toss to coat evenly. Gently stir in cucumber and cheese.

2. Arrange one lettuce leaf on each serving plate. Spoon salad evenly onto lettuce leaves. Top with basil, if desired.

CABBAGE AND RED POTATO SALAD WITH CILANTRO-LIME DRESSING

½ cup finely chopped fresh cilantro

2 tablespoons fresh lime juice

2 tablespoons olive oil

2 teaspoons honey

½ teaspoon ground cumin

¼ teaspoon salt

2 cups sliced napa cabbage

2 cups sliced red cabbage

12 ounces baby red potatoes (about 4 potatoes), quartered and cooked

½ cup sliced green onions

2 tablespoons sunflower kernels

1. For dressing, whisk cilantro, lime juice, oil, honey, cumin and salt in small bowl until smooth and well blended. Let stand 30 minutes to allow flavors to blend.

2. Combine napa cabbage, red cabbage, potatoes and green onions in large bowl; mix well. Add dressing; toss to coat. Sprinkle with sunflower kernels.

GREEK CHICKPEA SALAD

- 4 cups packed baby spinach leaves
- 1 cup cooked chickpeas
- 1 large shallot, thinly sliced
- 4 pitted kalamata olives, sliced
- 2 tablespoons crumbled feta cheese
- ¼ cup plain Greek yogurt
- 2 teaspoons white wine vinegar
- 1 small clove garlic, minced
- 1 tablespoon olive oil
- ¼ teaspoon salt
- ¼ teaspoon black pepper

1. Combine spinach, chickpeas, shallot, olives and feta cheese in large bowl; toss gently.

2. Whisk yogurt, vinegar, garlic, oil, salt and pepper in small bowl until well blended. Add to salad; toss gently.

PASTA DISHES

FETTUCCINE WITH PESTO

Makes 4 servings

1 pound uncooked
   whole wheat
   fettuccine

Pesto Sauce

1 cup packed fresh
   basil leaves

½ cup pine nuts,
   toasted*

2 cloves garlic

½ teaspoon salt

¼ teaspoon black
   pepper

¼ cup plus
   1 tablespoon olive
   oil, divided

*Place pine nuts in small
saucepan. Heat over low
heat 2 minutes or until light
brown and fragrant, shaking
occasionally.*

1. Bring large saucepan of water to a boil. Add pasta; cook according to package directions. Drain; set aside and keep warm.

2. Meanwhile for pesto sauce, place basil, pine nuts, garlic, salt and pepper in food processor; drizzle with 1 tablespoon oil. Process about 10 seconds or until coarsely chopped. With motor running, drizzle in remaining ¼ cup oil. Process about 30 seconds or until almost smooth. Toss with hot cooked pasta.

Note: Pesto can be made 1 week in advance. Store in covered container in refrigerator. Makes ½ cup pesto.

ORZO WITH BLACK BEANS AND EDAMAME

Makes 2 to 4 servings

⅔ cup uncooked orzo

¾ cup frozen shelled edamame

¾ cup diced carrots

¾ cup cooked black beans

½ cup diced green bell pepper

2 to 3 tablespoons lime juice

1 tablespoon extra virgin olive oil

½ teaspoon salt

⅛ teaspoon black pepper

2 tablespoons finely chopped fresh cilantro

2 tablespoons grated Parmesan cheese

1. Cook orzo according to package directions. About 5 minutes before end of cooking, add edamame and carrots; cook until orzo is tender. Drain and transfer to large bowl; add black beans and bell pepper.

2. For dressing, whisk lime juice, oil, salt and black pepper in small bowl. Pour over salad; sprinkle with cilantro and top with cheese. Toss gently to blend. Serve warm or cold.

LENTILS AND ORZO

Makes 4 servings

8 cups water

½ cup dried lentils, rinsed and sorted

4 ounces uncooked orzo

1½ cups quartered grape or cherry tomatoes

¾ cup finely chopped celery

½ cup chopped red onion

2 ounces pitted olives (about 16 olives), coarsely chopped

3 to 4 tablespoons cider vinegar

1 tablespoon olive oil

1 tablespoon dried basil

1 clove garlic, minced

⅛ teaspoon dried red pepper flakes

4 ounces feta cheese

1. Bring water to a boil in large saucepan over high heat. Add lentils; boil 12 minutes.

2. Add orzo; cook 10 minutes or until orzo and lentils are tender. Drain and rinse under cold water to cool completely.

3. Meanwhile, combine tomatoes, celery, red onion and olives in large bowl; stir in lentil mixture.

4. For dressing, whisk vinegar, oil, basil and red pepper flakes in small bowl. Pour over salad; toss to coat. Stir in cheese. Let stand 15 minutes before serving.

COLD PEANUT NOODLE AND EDAMAME SALAD

8 ounces uncooked whole wheat spaghetti

1 small seedless cucumber

2 large carrots

3 tablespoons soy sauce

2 tablespoons dark sesame oil

2 tablespoons unseasoned rice vinegar

1 tablespoon sugar

1 tablespoon finely grated fresh ginger

1 tablespoon creamy peanut butter

1 tablespoon sriracha or hot chili sauce

2 teaspoons minced garlic

½ cup thawed frozen shelled edamame

¼ cup sliced green onions

¼ cup chopped peanuts

1. Cook noodles according to package directions. Rinse under cold water; drain. Cut noodles into 3-inch lengths. Place in large bowl; set aside. Spiral cucumber and carrots with fine spiral blade of spiralizer or thinly slice lengthwise.

2. For dressing, whisk soy sauce, oil, vinegar, sugar, ginger, peanut butter, sriracha and garlic in small bowl until smooth and well blended.

3. Gently toss noodles with dressing. Stir in edamame, cucumber and carrots. Cover and refrigerate at least 30 minutes to allow flavors to blend.

4. Sprinkle with green onions and peanuts just before serving.

SPAGHETTI WITH PESTO TOFU SQUARES

Makes 4 servings

2 tablespoons olive oil

1 yellow onion, finely chopped

1 carrot, finely chopped

1 stalk celery, finely chopped

2 cloves garlic, minced

1 can (28 ounces) plum tomatoes, undrained

¼ cup packed chopped fresh basil leaves

Salt and black pepper

1 package (14 ounces) extra firm tofu

½ cup pesto sauce (page 64)

1 package (16 ounces) uncooked spaghetti

½ cup shredded Parmesan cheese

¼ cup pine nuts, toasted*

To toast nuts, place in nonstick skillet. Cook and stir 3 minutes over medium-low heat or until nuts begin to brown. Spread on plate to cool.

1. Heat oil in large saucepan over medium heat. Add onion, carrot, celery and garlic. Cover and cook about 5 minutes or until tender, stirring occasionally.

2. Drain tomatoes, reserving juice. Coarsely chop tomatoes or crush with fingers. Add tomatoes and reserved juice to saucepan; bring to a boil over high heat. Reduce heat to medium-low. Simmer, uncovered, about 45 minutes or until slightly thickened and reduced, stirring frequently. Stir in basil during last 5 minutes of cooking. Season with salt and pepper.

3. Meanwhile, preheat oven to 350°F. Spray shallow baking dish with nonstick cooking spray.

4. Cut tofu into 1-inch cubes. Combine tofu and pesto in medium bowl; toss to coat. Arrange in prepared baking dish. Bake 15 minutes.

5. Cook spaghetti according to package directions; drain and stir into sauce. Cover and cook 5 minutes over low heat or until hot. Serve with tofu, cheese and pine nuts.

VEGETARIAN RICE NOODLES

Makes 4 servings

½ cup soy sauce

⅓ cup sugar

¼ cup lime juice

2 fresh red Thai chiles *or* 1 large jalapeño pepper, finely chopped

8 ounces thin rice noodles (rice vermicelli)

¼ cup vegetable oil

8 ounces firm tofu, drained and cut into triangles

1 jicama, peeled and chopped *or* 1 can (8 ounces) sliced water chestnuts, drained

2 medium sweet potatoes, peeled, halved lengthwise and cut into ¼-inch-thick slices

2 large leeks, cut into ¼-inch-thick slices

¼ cup chopped dry-roasted peanuts

2 tablespoons chopped fresh mint

2 tablespoons chopped fresh cilantro

1. Combine soy sauce, sugar, lime juice and chiles in small bowl until well blended; set aside.

2. Place rice noodles in medium bowl. Cover with hot water; let stand 15 minutes or until soft. Drain well; cut into 3-inch lengths.

3. Meanwhile, heat oil in large skillet over medium-high heat. Add tofu; cook 3 minutes per side or until golden brown. Transfer to paper towel-lined baking sheet with slotted spoon.

4. Add jicama to skillet; stir-fry 5 minutes or until lightly browned. Remove to baking sheet. Stir-fry sweet potatoes in batches until tender and browned; remove to baking sheet. Add leeks; stir-fry 1 minute; remove to baking sheet.

5. Stir soy sauce mixture; add to skillet. Cook until sugar dissolves. Add noodles; toss to coat. Gently stir in tofu, vegetables, peanuts, mint and cilantro.

SPAGHETTI AND BEETS
AGLIO E OLIO

Makes 4 to 6 servings

2 medium beets, peeled

8 ounces uncooked spaghetti or thin spaghetti

⅓ cup plus 1 tablespoon olive oil, divided

1 cup fresh bread crumbs*

4 cloves garlic, very thinly sliced

¾ teaspoon salt

½ teaspoon red pepper flakes

½ cup chopped fresh Italian parsley

¾ cup shredded Parmesan cheese, divided

To make fresh bread crumbs, tear 2 ounces Italian or French bread into pieces; process in food processor until coarse crumbs form.

1. Spiral beets with fine spiral blade of spiralizer; cut into desired lengths. Cook spaghetti according to package directions. Drain and return to saucepan, reserving ½ cup water; keep warm.

2. Meanwhile, spray large nonstick skillet; heat over medium-high heat. Add beets; cook and stir 8 to 10 minutes or until tender.

3. Heat 1 tablespoon oil in large skillet over medium heat. Add bread crumbs; cook 4 to 5 minutes or until golden brown, stirring frequently. Transfer to small bowl.

4. Add remaining ⅓ cup oil, garlic, salt and red pepper flakes to same skillet; cook about 3 minutes or just until garlic begins to brown on edges.

5. Add pasta, beets and parsley to skillet; toss to coat with oil mixture. Add some of reserved pasta water to moisten pasta, if desired. Stir in bread crumbs and ½ cup cheese. Top with remaining ¼ cup cheese just before serving.

GRAIN AND LEGUME BOWLS

BULGUR PILAF WITH CARAMELIZED ONIONS AND KALE

Makes 2 to 4 servings

1 tablespoon olive oil

1 small onion, cut into thin wedges

1 clove garlic, minced

2 cups chopped kale

2 cups vegetable or chicken broth

¾ cup medium grain bulgur

½ teaspoon salt

¼ teaspoon black pepper

1. Heat oil in large nonstick skillet over medium heat. Add onion; cook about 8 minutes or until softened and lightly browned, stirring frequently. Add garlic; cook and stir 1 minute. Add kale; cook and stir about 1 minute or until kale is wilted.

2. Stir in broth, bulgur, salt and pepper. Bring to a boil. Reduce heat; cover and simmer 12 minutes or until liquid is absorbed and bulgur is tender.

GREEK LENTIL SALAD WITH FETA VINAIGRETTE

Makes 2 to 4 servings

4 cups water

¾ cup uncooked lentils

1 bay leaf

¼ cup chopped green onions

1 large stalk celery, chopped

1 cup grape tomatoes, halved

¼ cup crumbled feta cheese

2 tablespoons olive oil

1 tablespoon white wine vinegar

½ teaspoon dried thyme

½ teaspoon dried oregano

½ teaspoon salt

¼ teaspoon black pepper

1. Combine water, lentils and bay leaf in small saucepan. Bring to a boil. Reduce heat to medium-low; partially cover and cook 40 minutes or until lentils are tender but not mushy.

2. Drain lentils; remove and discard bay leaf. Place lentils in serving bowl; stir in green onions, celery and tomatoes.

3. Combine feta, oil, vinegar, thyme, oregano, salt and pepper in small bowl. Pour over salad; gently stir until blended. Let stand at least 10 minutes before serving to allow flavors to blend.

FENNEL WHEAT BERRY SALAD

3 cups water

½ cup uncooked
     wheat berries

½ teaspoon salt

2 tablespoons
     balsamic vinegar

1 tablespoon olive oil

1 tablespoon honey

1¼ teaspoons whole
        fennel seeds,
        toasted (optional)

2 cups shredded
     red and/or green
     cabbage*

1 cup matchstick
     carrots*

*Or substitute 3 cups
coleslaw mix.

1. Combine water, wheat berries and salt in medium saucepan. Bring to a boil. Reduce heat; cover and simmer about 1 hour or until wheat berries are tender. Drain off any water. Place wheat berries in large bowl; cover and refrigerate at least 1 hour.

2. For dressing, whisk vinegar, oil, honey and fennel seeds, if desired, in small bowl.

3. Add cabbage and carrots to wheat berries. Drizzle with dressing; toss to coat. Serve immediately.

FRUIT AND NUT QUINOA

Makes 4 to 6 servings

1 cup uncooked quinoa

2 cups water

2 tablespoons finely grated orange peel, plus additional for garnish

¼ cup fresh orange juice

1 tablespoon olive oil

½ teaspoon salt

¼ teaspoon ground cinnamon

⅓ cup dried cranberries

⅓ cup toasted pistachio nuts*

*To toast nuts, place in nonstick skillet. Cook and stir 5 minutes over medium-low heat or until nuts begin to brown. Spread on plate to cool.

1. Place quinoa in fine-mesh strainer; rinse well under cold running water. Bring 2 cups water to a boil in small saucepan; stir in quinoa. Reduce heat to low; cover and simmer 10 to 15 minutes or until quinoa is tender and water is absorbed. Stir in 2 tablespoons orange peel.

2. Whisk orange juice, oil, salt and cinnamon in small bowl. Pour over quinoa; gently toss to coat. Fold in cranberries and pistachios. Serve warm or at room temperature. Garnish with additional orange peel.

BULGUR WITH ASPARAGUS AND SPRING HERBS

Makes 2 to 4 servings

⅔ cup uncooked bulgur

2 cups sliced asparagus (1-inch pieces)

½ cup frozen peas, thawed

⅔ cup chopped fresh Italian parsley

2 teaspoons finely chopped fresh mint

3 tablespoons lemon juice

1 tablespoon orange juice

1 tablespoon extra virgin olive oil

½ teaspoon salt

⅛ teaspoon black pepper

1. Prepare bulgur according to package directions. Drain well; place in large bowl.

2. Steam asparagus in steamer basket over boiling water 3 to 4 minutes or until bright green and crisp-tender. Run under cold water to stop cooking. Add to bowl with bulgur. Stir in peas, parsley and mint.

3. Whisk lemon juice, orange juice, oil, salt and pepper in small bowl. Pour over salad; toss gently.

BROWN RICE WITH ASPARAGUS AND TOMATOES

Makes 4 servings

1 cup uncooked brown rice

12 medium asparagus, cooked and cut into 1-inch pieces

2 medium tomatoes

3 tablespoons olive oil

2 tablespoons lemon juice

½ teaspoon salt

⅛ teaspoon black pepper

¼ cup minced fresh chives or green onions

2 teaspoons minced fresh dill

1. Cook rice according to package directions. Fluff with fork; set aside.

2. Meanwhile, place asparagus in large bowl. Core tomatoes over a separate bowl to catch juice. Dice tomatoes, reserving juice. Add tomatoes to asparagus. Whisk 1½ tablespoons reserved tomato juice, oil, lemon juice, salt and pepper in small bowl until well blended. Stir in chives and dill.

3. Add rice to asparagus. Pour in dressing; toss lightly to coat.

QUINOA WITH TOMATO, BROCCOLI AND FETA

Makes 2 to 4 servings

⅔ cup uncooked quinoa

2 cups water

2 cups small broccoli florets

1 plum tomato, diced

⅓ cup crumbled feta cheese

2 tablespoons lemon juice

1 tablespoon extra virgin olive oil

¼ teaspoon dried dill weed or basil

¼ teaspoon salt

⅛ teaspoon black pepper

1. Place quinoa in fine-mesh strainer; rinse well under cold water. Bring 2 cups water to a boil in small saucepan; stir in quinoa. Reduce heat to low; cover and simmer 10 to 15 minutes or until quinoa is tender and water is absorbed. Transfer to large bowl; cool to lukewarm.

2. Steam broccoli in steamer basket over boiling water 3 minutes or until just tender. Add to quinoa. Stir in tomatoes and cheese.

3. For dressing, whisk lemon juice, oil, dill, salt and pepper in small bowl. Pour over salad; toss gently.

SAVORY WILD RICE SALAD

Makes 6 to 8 servings

1 cup uncooked wild rice blend

½ cup coarsely chopped pecans or hazelnuts

¼ cup chopped sun-dried tomatoes (not packed in oil)

¼ cup chopped fresh chives or freeze-dried chives

1 tablespoon chopped fresh parsley

¼ teaspoon plus ¾ teaspoon salt, divided

¼ teaspoon dried thyme

½ teaspoon black pepper, divided

1 red bell pepper, finely diced

¼ cup finely chopped green onions

1 tablespoon white wine vinegar

3 tablespoons olive oil

1. Cook wild rice blend according to package directions, adding pecans, tomatoes, chives, parsley, ¼ teaspoon salt, thyme and ¼ teaspoon black pepper during last 10 minutes of cooking.

2. Transfer to large bowl; cool to room temperature. Stir in bell pepper and green onions.

3. Combine vinegar, remaining ¾ teaspoon salt and remaining ¼ teaspoon black pepper in small bowl, stirring until salt dissolves. Whisk in oil. Add to salad; stir until well blended.

Note: If you can't find a premixed wild rice blend or prefer to buy your rice in bulk, use ½ cup wild rice and ½ cup long grain brown rice instead. Bring 2 cups water and rice to a boil in medium saucepan over high heat. Reduce heat to low; cover and simmer about 50 minutes or until rice is tender. Remove from heat; let stand, covered, 10 minutes.

BARLEY SALAD

2 cups water

1 cup quick-cooking barley

½ cup dried currants

½ cup chopped pecans

⅓ cup chopped fresh chives

¾ teaspoon salt

½ teaspoon ground cumin

¼ to ½ teaspoon black pepper

1 cup finely chopped celery

1 red bell pepper, finely chopped

2½ tablespoons olive oil

1 tablespoon white wine vinegar

Chopped green onions (optional)

1. Bring water to a boil in medium saucepan. Add barley, currants, pecans and chives; stir well. Cover and reduce heat to low. Simmer 10 minutes or until barley is tender. Remove from heat. Cover and let stand 10 minutes or until water is absorbed.

2. Transfer to large bowl. Stir in salt, cumin and black pepper. Let stand until barley is lukewarm.

3. Stir in celery, bell pepper, oil and vinegar. Garnish with green onions. Serve at room temperature.

BULGUR SALAD NIÇOISE

2 cups water

¼ teaspoon salt

1 cup bulgur wheat

1 cup halved cherry tomatoes

1 can (6 ounces) tuna packed in water, drained and flaked

½ cup pitted black niçoise olives

3 tablespoons finely chopped green onions

1 tablespoon chopped fresh mint

1½ tablespoons lemon juice, or to taste

1 tablespoon olive oil

⅛ teaspoon black pepper

1. Bring water and salt to a boil in medium saucepan. Stir in bulgur. Remove from heat. Cover and let stand 10 to 15 minutes or until water is absorbed and bulgur is tender. Fluff with fork; cool completely.

2. Combine bulgur, tomatoes, tuna, olives, green onions and chopped mint in large bowl.

3. Combine lemon juice, oil and pepper in small bowl. Pour over salad. Toss gently to mix well.

BULGUR, GREEN BEAN AND ORANGE SALAD

Makes 2 to 4 servings

⅔ cup bulgur

⅔ cup boiling water

1½ cups green beans, cut into 1-inch pieces

2 tablespoons olive oil

2 tablespoons lemon juice

½ teaspoon Greek seasoning

¼ teaspoon salt

¼ teaspoon black pepper

1 can (11 ounces) mandarin orange sections, drained

¼ cup slivered red onion

4 cups packed fresh baby spinach

1. Place bulgur in medium bowl. Pour boiling water over bulgur; stir. Cover and let stand 20 minutes or until bulgur is tender.

2. Meanwhile, cook beans in boiling water in small saucepan 6 to 7 minutes or until tender; drain.

3. For dressing, combine oil, lemon juice, Greek seasoning, salt and pepper in small bowl; whisk until well blended.

4. Add beans, orange sections and onion to bulgur. Drizzle with dressing; toss until well blended. Cover and refrigerate at least 30 minutes.

5. Place spinach in large bowl. Add salad; toss to blend.

GREEK RICE SALAD

Makes 2 servings

1½ cups water

½ cup uncooked long grain brown rice

1 cup packed fresh baby spinach

⅔ cup quartered cherry tomatoes

1 tablespoon lemon juice

1 tablespoon extra virgin olive oil

1½ teaspoons Greek seasoning

¼ teaspoon salt

⅛ teaspoon black pepper

¼ cup pine nuts

1. Bring water to a boil in small saucepan over high heat; add rice. Reduce heat to low; cover and simmer 45 minutes or until rice is tender. Drain and rinse under cold water to cool.

2. Combine spinach, tomatoes and rice in medium bowl. Whisk lemon juice, oil, Greek seasoning, salt and pepper in small bowl.

3. Pour dressing over salad; toss to blend. Serve immediately or refrigerate until ready to serve. Sprinkle with pine nuts just before serving.

BARLEY AND SWISS CHARD SKILLET CASSEROLE

Makes 4 servings

1 cup water

1 cup chopped red bell pepper

1 cup chopped green bell pepper

¾ cup uncooked quick-cooking barley

¼ teaspoon salt

⅛ teaspoon garlic powder

⅛ teaspoon red pepper flakes

2 cups packed coarsely chopped Swiss chard*

1 cup cooked navy beans

1 cup quartered cherry tomatoes

¼ cup chopped fresh basil

1 tablespoon olive oil

2 tablespoons fine fresh bread crumbs

Fresh spinach or beet greens can be substituted for Swiss chard.

1. Preheat broiler.

2. Bring water to a boil in large ovenproof skillet; add bell peppers, barley, salt, garlic powder and red pepper flakes. Reduce heat; cover and simmer 10 minutes or until liquid is absorbed. Remove from heat.

3. Stir in chard, beans, tomatoes, basil and oil. Sprinkle with bread crumbs. Broil 2 minutes or until golden.

QUINOA AND MANGO SALAD

Makes 4 to 6 servings

1 cup uncooked quinoa

2 cups water

2 cups cubed peeled mango (about 2 large mangoes)

½ cup sliced green onions

½ cup dried cranberries

2 tablespoons chopped fresh parsley

¼ cup extra virgin olive oil

1 tablespoon plus 1½ teaspoons white wine vinegar

1 teaspoon Dijon mustard

½ teaspoon salt

⅛ teaspoon black pepper

1. Place quinoa in fine-mesh strainer; rinse well under cold running water. Combine quinoa and 2 cups water in medium saucepan; bring to a boil over high heat. Reduce heat to low; cover and simmer 10 to 12 minutes until quinoa is tender and water is absorbed. Stir quinoa; let stand, covered, 15 minutes. Transfer to large bowl; cover and refrigerate at least 1 hour.

2. Add mangoes, green onions, cranberries and parsley to quinoa; mix well.

3. Combine oil, vinegar, mustard, salt and pepper in small bowl; whisk until blended. Pour over quinoa mixture; mix until well blended.

SOUTHWESTERN CHILE BEAN SALAD

Makes 2 to 4 servings

2 cups cooked pinto beans

1 jalapeño pepper, seeded and minced

2 medium tomatoes, diced

½ cup chopped green onions

1 stalk celery, thinly sliced

2 tablespoons tomato juice

4 teaspoons red wine vinegar

2 teaspoons canola oil

½ teaspoon paprika

¼ teaspoon ground cumin

¼ teaspoon salt

¼ teaspoon black pepper

½ cup (2 ounces) shredded sharp Cheddar cheese

1. Combine beans, jalapeño pepper, tomatoes, green onions and celery in large bowl.

2. Whisk tomato juice, vinegar, oil, paprika, cumin, salt and black pepper in small bowl. Pour over salad; toss to coat. Sprinkle with cheese.

FRUITY WILD RICE PILAF

1 cup uncooked wild rice blend*

½ cup finely chopped dried apricots

⅓ cup coarsely chopped hazelnuts

6 tablespoons chopped fresh Italian parsley

¼ teaspoon curry powder

¼ teaspoon ground cumin

¼ teaspoon black pepper

Pinch ground red pepper

1½ cups finely shredded or chopped red cabbage

1½ tablespoons white wine vinegar

1 tablespoon honey

½ teaspoon salt

1½ tablespoons vegetable oil

See note on page 94.

1. Cook wild rice blend according to package directions, adding apricots, hazelnuts, parsley, curry powder, cumin, black pepper and ground red pepper during last 10 minutes of cooking.

2. Transfer to large bowl; cool to room temperature. Stir in cabbage.

3. Whisk vinegar, honey and salt in small bowl until well blended. Whisk in oil. Pour over salad; toss to coat.

VEGETABLE SIDES AND SNACKS

BUTTERNUT SQUASH OVEN CHIPS

Makes 4 servings

Lime Yogurt Dip (recipe follows)

½ teaspoon garlic powder

¼ teaspoon salt

¼ teaspoon ground red pepper

1 butternut squash (about 2½ pounds), peeled and seeded and cut in half lengthwise

2 teaspoons vegetable oil

1. Preheat oven to 425°F. Prepare Lime Yogurt Dip. Combine garlic powder, salt and ground red pepper in small bowl.

2. Cut squash crosswise into ¼-inch slices. Spread squash on baking sheet. Drizzle with oil and sprinkle with seasoning mix; gently toss to coat. Arrange in single layer.

3. Bake 20 to 25 minutes or until squash is browned and crisp, turning occasionally.

Lime Yogurt Dip: Combine ¼ cup mayonnaise, ¼ cup plain Greek yogurt, 1 teaspoon lime juice and ¼ teaspoon grated lime peel in small bowl. Refrigerate until ready to serve.

OVEN-ROASTED ASPARAGUS

1 bunch (about 12 ounces) fresh asparagus spears

1 tablespoon olive oil

½ teaspoon salt

¼ teaspoon black pepper

¼ cup shredded Asiago or Parmesan cheese (optional)

1. Preheat oven to 425°F.

2. Trim off and discard tough ends of asparagus spears. Peel stem ends with vegetable peeler, if desired. Arrange asparagus in shallow baking dish; drizzle with oil, turning spears to coat. Sprinkle with salt and pepper.

3. Roast 12 to 18 minutes or until asparagus is tender. Chop or leave spears whole. Sprinkle with cheese, if desired.

VEGETABLE-TOPPED HUMMUS

Makes 8 servings

2 cups cooked chickpeas

2 tablespoons tahini

2 tablespoons lemon juice

1 clove garlic

¾ teaspoon salt

1 tomato, finely chopped

2 green onions, finely chopped

2 tablespoons chopped fresh parsley

Pita bread rounds or assorted crackers (optional)

1. Combine chickpeas, tahini, lemon juice, garlic and salt in food processor or blender; process until smooth.

2. Combine tomato, green onions and parsley in small bowl; toss gently to combine.

3. Spoon hummus into serving bowl; top with tomato mixture. Serve with pita bread rounds or assorted crackers, if desired.

KALE CHIPS

1 large bunch kale (about 1 pound)

1 to 2 tablespoons olive oil

1 teaspoon garlic salt or other seasoned salt

1. Preheat oven to 350°F. Line baking sheets with parchment paper.

2. Wash kale and pat dry with paper towels. Remove center ribs and stems; discard. Cut leaves into 2- to 3-inch-wide pieces.

3. Combine leaves, oil and garlic salt in large bowl; toss to coat. Spread on prepared baking sheets.

4. Bake 10 to 15 minutes or until edges are lightly browned and leaves are crisp.* Cool completely on baking sheets. Store in airtight container.

*If the leaves are lightly browned but not crisp, turn oven off and let chips stand in oven until crisp, about 10 minutes. Do not keep the oven on as the chips will burn easily.

CURLY CURRY CHIPS

4 small or 2 large russet potatoes, peeled

1 teaspoon vegetable oil

¾ teaspoon salt, divided

1 tablespoon butter

¼ cup finely chopped onion

1 tablespoon all-purpose flour

1 tablespoon curry powder

1 cup vegetable broth

1. Preheat oven to 450°F. Line large baking sheet with parchment paper. Spiral potatoes with thick spiral blade of spiralizer. Spread potatoes on prepared baking sheet; drizzle with oil. Bake 30 to 35 minutes or until golden brown and crispy, turning once. Sprinkle with ½ teaspoon salt.

2. Melt butter in small saucepan over medium-high heat. Add onion; cook and stir about 3 minutes or until softened. Whisk in flour and curry powder until well blended; cook 1 minute, stirring constantly. Add broth in thin steady stream, whisking constantly.

3. Reduce heat to medium; cook about 10 minutes or until thick. Taste and add remaining ¼ teaspoon salt, if desired. For smoother sauce, cool slightly and purée in blender or food processor. Serve with potatoes.

Note: If you don't have a spiralizer, cut potatoes into ¼-inch-thick sticks with sharp knife or mandoline.

CARAMELIZED BRUSSELS SPROUTS WITH CRANBERRIES

Makes 4 servings

1 tablespoon vegetable oil

1 pound Brussels sprouts, ends trimmed and discarded, thinly sliced

¼ cup dried cranberries

2 teaspoons packed brown sugar

¼ teaspoon salt

1. Heat oil in large skillet over medium-high heat. Add Brussels sprouts; cook and stir 10 minutes or until crisp-tender and beginning to brown.

2. Add cranberries, brown sugar and salt; cook and stir 5 minutes or until browned.

BITE-YOU-BACK ROASTED EDAMAME

2 teaspoons vegetable oil

2 teaspoons honey

¼ teaspoon wasabi powder

1 package (10 ounces) shelled edamame, thawed if frozen

Kosher salt (optional)

1. Preheat oven to 375°F.

2. Combine oil, honey and wasabi powder in large bowl; mix well. Add edamame; toss to coat. Spread in single layer on baking sheet.

3. Bake 12 to 15 minutes or until golden brown, stirring once. Immediately remove from baking sheet to large bowl; sprinkle generously with salt, if desired. Cool completely before serving. Store in airtight container.

APPLE SALSA

1 cup finely chopped unpeeled red apples

¼ cup finely chopped red onion

¼ cup minced Anaheim pepper

½ jalapeño pepper, seeded and minced

2 tablespoons lime juice

1 teaspoon chopped fresh cilantro

¼ teaspoon black pepper

⅛ teaspoon salt

Tortilla chips

1. Combine apples, onion, Anaheim and jalapeño peppers, lime juice, cilantro, black pepper and salt in large bowl; mix well. Cover and refrigerate at least 30 minutes or overnight.

2. Serve with tortilla chips.

CREAMED KALE

2 pounds kale

2 tablespoons butter

2 tablespoons all-purpose flour

1½ cups milk

½ cup shredded Parmesan cheese, plus additional for garnish

2 cloves garlic, minced

¼ teaspoon salt

⅛ teaspoon ground nutmeg

1. Remove stems from kale; discard. Coarsely chop leaves. Bring large saucepan of water to a boil. Add kale; cook 5 minutes. Drain.

2. Melt butter in large saucepan over medium heat. Stir in flour. Cook and stir 1 to 2 minutes or until smooth. Gradually whisk in milk until well blended. Whisk constantly over medium heat 4 to 5 minutes or until sauce boils and thickens. Whisk in ½ cup cheese, garlic, salt and nutmeg.

3. Remove saucepan from heat. Fold in kale until combined. Sprinkle with additional cheese, if desired.

BEET NOODLES WITH EDAMAME, SPINACH AND FETA

Makes 4 servings

4 medium beets
   (2 each red and
   golden)

1 onion

2 tablespoons olive
   oil, divided

1 cup frozen shelled
   edamame

¾ cup water

¾ teaspoon dried
   herbes de
   Provence

¼ teaspoon salt

⅛ teaspoon black
   pepper

6 ounces fresh spinach
   (about 8 cups), torn
   into small pieces
   and rinsed

¾ cup (3 ounces)
   crumbled feta
   cheese

1. Spiral beets and onion with thin spiral blade of spiralizer; cut into desired lengths.

2. Heat 1 tablespoon oil in large skillet over medium heat. Add beets; cook and stir 7 to 10 minutes or until tender. Transfer to large bowl.

3. Heat remaining 1 tablespoon oil in same skillet. Add onion; cook and stir 4 minutes or until lightly browned. Stir in edamame, water, herbes de Provence, salt and pepper. Reduce heat; cover and simmer 7 minutes.

4. Add spinach with water clinging to leaves; cover and cook 8 minutes or until spinach is tender. Add to beets; mix well. Sprinkle with cheese just before serving.

GRILLED SESAME ASPARAGUS

Makes 4 servings

1 pound medium asparagus spears (about 20), trimmed

1 tablespoon vegetable oil

1 tablespoon sesame seeds

2 to 3 teaspoons balsamic vinegar

¼ teaspoon salt

¼ teaspoon black pepper

1. Spray grid with nonstick cooking spray; prepare grill for direct cooking.

2. Place asparagus on baking sheet; drizzle with oil. Sprinkle with sesame seeds, rolling to coat.

3. Place asparagus on grid. Grill, uncovered, 4 to 6 minutes or until the asparagus begins to brown, turning once.

4. Transfer asparagus to serving dish. Sprinkle with vinegar, salt and pepper.

Tip: Be sure to use the entire amount of pepper—it really brings out the flavors of this dish.

SPANISH RICE-STYLE RUTABAGA WITH AVOCADO

Makes 4 to 6 servings

1 large rutabaga, peeled

1 onion

2 tablespoons olive oil

1 clove garlic, minced

½ teaspoon salt

½ teaspoon dried oregano

½ teaspoon ground cumin

½ teaspoon ground turmeric

1 can (about 14 ounces) vegetable broth

1 avocado, diced

1. Spiral rutabaga with thick spiral blade of spiralizer. Place in food processor; pulse until small pieces form. Spiral onion with fine spiral blade; cut into desired lengths.

2. Heat oil in medium saucepan over medium heat. Add onion and garlic; cook and stir until onion is tender. Add rutabaga, salt, oregano, cumin, turmeric and broth; bring to a boil. Reduce heat; cover and cook 10 minutes or until rutabaga is tender. Remove from heat; stir in avocado.

KALE WITH LEMON AND GARLIC

2 bunches kale or Swiss chard (1 to 1¼ pounds)

1 tablespoon olive or vegetable oil

3 cloves garlic, minced

½ cup vegetable broth

½ teaspoon salt

¼ teaspoon black pepper

1 lemon, cut into 8 wedges

1. Trim any tough stems from kale. Stack and thinly slice leaves. Heat oil in large saucepan over medium heat. Add garlic; cook 3 minutes, stirring occasionally. Add chopped kale and broth; cover and simmer 7 minutes. Stir kale. Reduce heat to medium-low; cover and simmer 8 to 10 minutes or until kale is tender.

2. Stir in salt and pepper. Squeeze wedge of lemon over each serving.

ROASTED CARROT, POTATO AND ONION MELANGE

Makes 2 servings

4 ounces carrots

4 ounces yellow onion

4 ounces red potatoes

1 tablespoon sesame oil

½ teaspoon dried thyme

½ teaspoon salt

¼ teaspoon black pepper

1. Preheat oven to 425°F. Line baking sheet with parchment paper.

2. Spiral carrots and onion with fine spiral blade and spiral potatoes with medium spiral blade of spiralizer; cut vegetables into desired lengths. Spread on prepared baking sheet. Drizzle with sesame oil and sprinkle with thyme, salt and pepper; toss to coat. Arrange in single layer.

3. Bake 15 to 17 minutes or until edges of vegetables begin to brown, stirring occasionally.

Note: If you don't have a spiralizer, cut the vegetables into julienne strips.

BROCCOLI ITALIAN-STYLE

Makes 4 servings

1¼ pounds fresh broccoli

2 tablespoons lemon juice

1 teaspoon extra virgin olive oil

1 clove garlic, minced

1 teaspoon chopped fresh Italian parsley

½ teaspoon salt

Dash black pepper

1. Trim broccoli, discarding tough stems. Cut broccoli into florets with 2-inch stems. Peel remaining stems; cut into ½-inch slices.

2. Bring large pot of salted water to a boil over medium-high heat. Add broccoli; return to a boil. Cook 3 to 5 minutes or until broccoli is tender. Drain; transfer to serving dish.

3. Combine lemon juice, oil, garlic, parsley, salt and pepper in small bowl. Pour over broccoli; toss to coat. Cover and let stand 1 hour before serving to allow flavors to blend. Serve at room temperature.

HONEYED BEETS

1 medium red beet
   (8 ounces)

1 medium golden
   beet (8 ounces)

1 tablespoon
   vegetable oil

¼ cup unsweetened
   apple juice

2 tablespoons cider
   vinegar

1 tablespoon honey

2 teaspoons
   cornstarch

   Salt and black
   pepper

1. Preheat oven to 425°F. Line baking sheet with parchment paper.

2. Spiral beets with fine spiral blade of spiralizer; cut into desired lengths. Spread on prepared baking sheet, keeping golden beets separate from red beets; drizzle with oil. Bake 15 minutes or until tender, stirring occasionally.

3. Combine apple juice, vinegar, honey and cornstarch in large nonstick saucepan. Cook over medium heat until shimmering, stirring occasionally. Stir in beets; season to taste with salt and pepper. Simmer 3 minutes or until glazed.

CRUNCHY ASPARAGUS

1 bunch fresh asparagus (about 12 ounces)

1 teaspoon lemon juice

3 to 4 drops hot pepper sauce

¼ teaspoon salt

¼ teaspoon dried basil

⅛ teaspoon black pepper

2 teaspoons sunflower kernels

Lemon slices (optional)

1. Steam asparagus over boiling water until crisp-tender.

2. Combine lemon juice, hot pepper sauce, salt, basil and pepper in small bowl. Pour mixture over asparagus; toss to coat. Sprinkle with sunflower kernels. Garnish with lemon slices.

HOT BOWLS

FRENCH LENTIL RICE SOUP

6 cups vegetable broth

1 cup dried lentils, rinsed and sorted

2 carrots, finely diced

1 onion, finely chopped

2 stalks celery, finely diced

3 tablespoons uncooked rice

2 teaspoons minced garlic

1 teaspoon herbes de Provence

½ teaspoon salt

⅛ teaspoon black pepper

4 tablespoons whipping cream or sour cream

¼ cup chopped fresh parsley

Slow Cooker Directions

1. Combine broth, lentils, carrots, onion, celery, rice, garlic, herbes de Provence, salt and pepper in 5-quart slow cooker; stir well. Cover; cook on LOW 8 hours or on HIGH 4 hours.

2. Transfer about 1½ cups soup to blender or food processor; process until almost smooth. Return to slow cooker.

3. Ladle soup into bowls. Top with cream and with parsley.

QUICK BROCCOLI SOUP

Makes 4 servings

4 cups vegetable broth

2½ pounds broccoli florets

1 onion, quartered

1 cup milk

¼ teaspoon salt

¼ cup crumbled blue cheese

1. Place broth, broccoli and onion in large saucepan; bring to a boil over high heat. Reduce heat to low; cover and simmer about 20 minutes or until vegetables are tender.

2. Purée soup in batches in blender or food processor. Return to saucepan. Add milk and salt. Add water or additional broth if needed for desired consistency.

3. Ladle soup into serving bowls; sprinkle with cheese.

CURRIED COCONUT LENTIL SOUP

Makes 4 servings

1 tablespoon vegetable oil

1½ cups dried red lentils, rinsed and sorted

¼ cup minced onion

¼ cup unsweetened shredded coconut, plus additional for garnish

3 tablespoons curry powder

2 tablespoons fresh parsley, chopped

1 teaspoon ground ginger

½ teaspoon garlic powder

½ teaspoon salt

½ teaspoon black pepper

6 cups vegetable broth

2 cups water

1. Heat oil in large saucepan over medium heat. Add lentils, onion, ¼ cup coconut, curry powder, parsley, ginger, garlic powder, salt and pepper; cook and stir 1 minute or until spices are fragrant.

2. Add broth and water; bring to a boil over high heat. Reduce heat to low. Simmer, uncovered, 20 minutes or until lentils are tender. Garnish with additional coconut.

HEARTY WHITE BEAN MINESTRONE

Makes 6 servings

1 tablespoon olive oil

1 medium onion, chopped

3 medium carrots, chopped

3 medium stalks celery, chopped

2 cloves garlic, minced

2 medium russet potatoes (about 6 ounces each), peeled and cut into ½-inch cubes

5 cups vegetable broth

4 cups cooked cannellini beans

1 can (about 14 ounces) diced tomatoes

½ teaspoon dried oregano

½ teaspoon salt

½ teaspoon black pepper

6 cups chopped fresh kale

6 tablespoons shredded Parmesan cheese

1. Heat oil in large saucepan or Dutch oven over medium heat. Add onion, carrots, celery and garlic; cook and stir 10 minutes or until vegetables are softened.

2. Add potatoes, broth, beans, tomatoes, oregano, salt and pepper. Bring to a boil. Reduce heat; simmer 20 minutes. Stir in kale; cook 15 to 20 minutes or until kale is wilted and tender.

3. Ladle into bowls; top with cheese.

MIDDLE EASTERN LENTIL SOUP

Makes 4 servings

1 cup dried lentils

2 tablespoons olive oil

1 small onion, chopped

1 medium red bell pepper, chopped

1 teaspoon whole fennel seeds

½ teaspoon ground cumin

¼ teaspoon ground red pepper

4 cups water

½ teaspoon salt

1 tablespoon lemon juice

½ cup plain low-fat yogurt

2 tablespoons chopped fresh parsley

1. Rinse lentils, discarding any debris or blemished lentils; drain.

2. Heat oil in large saucepan over medium-high heat until hot. Add onion and bell pepper; cook and stir 5 minutes or until tender. Add fennel seeds, cumin and ground red pepper; cook and stir 1 minute.

3. Add water, lentils and salt. Bring to a boil. Reduce heat to low. Cover and simmer 25 to 30 minutes or until lentils are tender. Stir in lemon juice.

4. Ladle soup into individual bowls and top with yogurt; sprinkle with parsley.

CHICKPEA-VEGETABLE SOUP

Makes 4 servings

1 teaspoon olive oil

1 cup chopped onion

½ cup chopped green bell pepper

2 cloves garlic, minced

2 cans (about 14 ounces each) chopped tomatoes

3 cups water

2 cups broccoli florets

1½ cups cooked chickpeas, slightly mashed

½ cup uncooked orzo

1 whole bay leaf

1 tablespoon chopped fresh thyme *or* 1 teaspoon dried thyme

1 tablespoon chopped fresh rosemary leaves *or* 1 teaspoon dried rosemary

1 tablespoon lime or lemon juice

½ teaspoon ground turmeric

¼ teaspoon salt

¼ teaspoon ground red pepper

¼ cup pumpkin seeds

1. Heat oil in large saucepan over medium heat. Add onion, bell pepper and garlic; cook and stir 5 minutes or until vegetables are tender.

2. Add tomatoes, water, broccoli, chickpeas, orzo, bay leaf, thyme, rosemary, lime juice, turmeric, salt and ground red pepper. Bring to a boil over high heat. Reduce heat to medium-low; cover and simmer 10 to 12 minutes or until orzo is tender.

3. Remove and discard bay leaf. Ladle soup into bowls; sprinkle with pumpkin seeds.

SWEET RED BELL PEPPER SOUP

Makes 8 servings

8 red bell peppers

2 tablespoons olive oil

1 onion, thinly sliced

3 cloves garlic, minced

1 teaspoon black pepper

1 teaspoon dried oregano

½ teaspoon salt

2 tablespoons balsamic vinegar

2 teaspoons sugar

1½ tablespoons fresh thyme, divided

Slow Cooker Directions

1. Cut peppers in half and remove stem and seeds; slice into quarters. Coat slow cooker with oil. Add bell peppers, onion, garlic, black pepper, oregano and salt; gently mix. Cover; cook on HIGH 4 hours or until bell peppers are very tender; stirring halfway through cooking.

2. Purée soup in slow cooker using hand-held immersion blender. Or transfer mixture in batches to blender or food processor. Blend until smooth. Stir in balsamic vinegar and sugar. Ladle soup into bowls; garnish with thyme.

SWEET POTATO MINESTRONE

- 1 tablespoon extra virgin olive oil
- ¾ cup diced onion
- ½ cup diced celery
- 3 cups water
- 2 cups diced peeled sweet potatoes
- 1½ cups cooked Great Northern beans
- 1 can (about 14 ounces) diced tomatoes
- ¾ teaspoon dried rosemary
- ½ teaspoon salt
- ⅛ teaspoon black pepper
- 2 cups coarsely chopped kale leaves
- 4 tablespoons grated Parmesan cheese

1. Heat oil in large saucepan or Dutch oven over medium-high heat. Add onion and celery; cook and stir 4 minutes or until onion is softened. Stir water, sweet potatoes, beans, tomatoes, rosemary, salt and pepper into saucepan. Cover and bring to a simmer; reduce heat and simmer 30 minutes.

2. Add kale; cover and cook 10 minutes or until tender.

3. Ladle soup into bowls; sprinkle with cheese.

KALE AND WHITE BEAN SOUP

Makes 4 servings

- 1 tablespoon olive oil
- ½ cup diced onion
- 1 unpeeled new red potato, diced
- 4 cups vegetable broth
- 4 cups chopped kale leaves
- 1½ cups sliced carrots
- 1 teaspoon minced garlic
- ½ teaspoon salt
- ½ teaspoon dried oregano
- ¼ teaspoon black pepper
- 2 bay leaves
- 1½ cups cooked cannellini beans
- ⅓ cup finely chopped sun-dried tomato strips, packed in olive oil

1. Heat oil in large saucepan over medium heat. Add onion and potato; cook and stir 10 minutes or until onion is browned. Stir in broth, kale, carrots, garlic, salt, oregano, pepper and bay leaves; bring to a simmer. Cover and simmer 5 minutes or until potato is tender.

2. Add beans and sun-dried tomatoes; cook 5 minutes or until kale is tender. Remove and discard bay leaves.

HEARTY LENTIL AND ROOT VEGETABLE STEW

Makes 8 servings

4 cups vegetable broth

1½ cups diced turnip

1 cup dried red lentils, rinsed and sorted

1 medium onion, cut into ½-inch wedges

2 medium carrots, cut into 1-inch pieces

1 medium red bell pepper, cut into 1-inch pieces

½ teaspoon dried oregano

⅛ teaspoon red pepper flakes

1 tablespoon olive oil

½ teaspoon salt

Finely chopped green onions and/or cooked crumbled bacon, (optional)

Slow Cooker Directions

1. Combine broth, turnip, lentils, onion, carrots, bell pepper, oregano and red pepper flakes in 4-quart slow cooker. Cover; cook on LOW 6 hours or on HIGH 3 hours or until lentils are tender.

2. Stir in oil and salt. Ladle into bowls; garnish as desired.

MINESTRONE SOUP

Makes 4 to 6 servings

¾ cup uncooked small shell pasta

4 cups vegetable broth

1 can (28 ounces) crushed tomatoes in tomato purée

1½ cups cooked white beans

2 carrots, diced

1 cup chopped broccoli

1 cup green beans (1-inch pieces)

1 red bell pepper, diced

4 to 6 teaspoons prepared pesto

1. Cook pasta according to package directions; drain.

2. Meanwhile, combine broth, tomatoes, beans and carrots in large saucepan; bring to a boil over high heat. Reduce heat to low; cover and simmer 3 to 5 minutes.

3. Add broccoli, green beans and bell pepper; bring to a boil over high heat. Reduce heat to medium-low; stir in pasta. Simmer, uncovered, until vegetables and pasta are tender.

4. Ladle soup into bowls; top each serving with about 1 teaspoon pesto.

ITALIAN VEGETABLE SOUP

2 tablespoons olive oil, divided

1 medium orange, red or yellow bell pepper, chopped

1 clove garlic, minced

2 cups water

1 can (about 14 ounces) diced tomatoes

1 medium zucchini, thinly sliced lengthwise

⅛ teaspoon red pepper flakes

1½ cups cooked navy beans

3 to 4 tablespoons chopped fresh basil

1 tablespoon balsamic vinegar

¾ teaspoon salt

1. Heat 1 tablespoon oil in large saucepan or Dutch oven over medium-high heat. Add bell pepper; cook and stir 4 minutes or until edges are browned. Add garlic; cook and stir 15 seconds. Add water, tomatoes, zucchini and red pepper flakes; bring to a boil over high heat. Reduce heat to low; cover and simmer 20 minutes.

2. Add beans, basil, remaining 1 tablespoon oil, vinegar and salt; simmer 5 minutes. Remove from heat; let stand, covered, 10 minutes before serving.

PESTO ZOODLES WITH POTATOES

Makes 6 servings

- 3 medium red potatoes
- 1 large zucchini
- ¾ cup frozen peas
- ½ cup pesto sauce (page 64)
- ¼ cup plus 2 tablespoons grated Parmesan cheese, divided
- ¼ teaspoon salt
- ¼ teaspoon black pepper

1. Spiral potatoes and zucchini with fine spiral blade of spiralizer; cut into desired lengths.

2. Bring medium saucepan of water to a boil. Add potatoes; cook 5 to 7 minutes or until tender, adding peas and zucchini during last 2 minutes of cooking. Drain well; return to saucepan. Stir in pesto, ¼ cup cheese, salt and pepper, tossing until blended.

3. Sprinkle with remaining 2 tablespoons cheese just before serving.

SMOOTHIES AND JUICES

TRIPLE GREEN SMOOTHIE

2 cups seedless green grapes

1 kiwi, peeled and quartered

½ avocado

Combine grapes, kiwi and avocado in blender; blend until smooth.

WORKOUT WARMUP JUICE

2 apples

2 kiwis, peeled

4 leaves kale

½ lime, peeled

Juice apples, kiwis, kale and lime. Stir.

APPLE-K JUICE

Makes 2 servings

1 kiwi, peeled

1 apple

4 leaves kale

1 stalk celery

½ lemon, peeled

Juice kiwi, apple, kale, celery and lemon. Stir.

SUPER C SMOOTHIE

⅔ cup water

2 navel oranges,
   peeled and seeded

2 cups frozen
   blackberries

2 cups baby kale

1 avocado

2 tablespoons honey

Combine water, oranges, blackberries, kale, avocado and honey in blender; blend until smooth.

WHEATGRASS BLAST

Makes 2 servings

2 apples

2 cups wheatgrass

1 lemon, peeled

6 springs fresh mint

Juice apples, wheatgrass, lemon and mint. Stir.

GREENS AND CITRUS JUICE

Makes 2 servings

2 oranges, peeled

1 grapefruit, peeled

1 zucchini

½ cup broccoli florets

½ inch fresh ginger,
  peeled

Juice oranges, grapefruit, zucchini, broccoli and ginger. Stir.

PEAR GINGER JUICE

Makes 2 servings

2 pears

1 cucumber

1 lemon, peeled

1 inch fresh ginger,
   peeled

Ice cubes

Juice pears, cucumber, lemon and
ginger. Stir. Serve over ice.

VITAMIN BLAST JUICE

Makes 2 servings

¼ cantaloupe, rind removed

1 orange, peeled

¼ papaya

2 leaves Swiss chard

Juice cantaloupe, orange, papaya and chard. Stir.

SHARP APPLE COOLER

Makes 3 servings

3 apples

1 cucumber

¼ cup fresh mint

1 inch fresh ginger,
   peeled

Juice apples, cucumber, mint and ginger. Stir.

GREEN MORNING JUICE

Makes 1 serving

2 cups fresh spinach

1 apple

1 carrot

1 stalk celery

¼ lemon, peeled

1 inch fresh ginger,
   peeled

Juice spinach, apple, carrot, celery, lemon and ginger. Stir.

SPICY GREEN APPLE JUICE

2 apples

1½ cups arugula

½ cup fresh cilantro

½ jalapeño pepper

1 cup coconut water

Juice apples, arugula, cilantro and jalapeño pepper. Stir in coconut water until well blended.

INDEX

METRIC CONVERSION CHART

VOLUME MEASUREMENTS (dry)

$1/8$ teaspoon = 0.5 mL
$1/4$ teaspoon = 1 mL
$1/2$ teaspoon = 2 mL
$3/4$ teaspoon = 4 mL
1 teaspoon = 5 mL
1 tablespoon = 15 mL
2 tablespoons = 30 mL
$1/4$ cup = 60 mL
$1/3$ cup = 75 mL
$1/2$ cup = 125 mL
$2/3$ cup = 150 mL
$3/4$ cup = 175 mL
1 cup = 250 mL
2 cups = 1 pint = 500 mL
3 cups = 750 mL
4 cups = 1 quart = 1 L

VOLUME MEASUREMENTS (fluid)

1 fluid ounce (2 tablespoons) = 30 mL
4 fluid ounces ($1/2$ cup) = 125 mL
8 fluid ounces (1 cup) = 250 mL
12 fluid ounces ($1 1/2$ cups) = 375 mL
16 fluid ounces (2 cups) = 500 mL

WEIGHTS (mass)

$1/2$ ounce = 15 g
1 ounce = 30 g
3 ounces = 90 g
4 ounces = 120 g
8 ounces = 225 g
10 ounces = 285 g
12 ounces = 360 g
16 ounces = 1 pound = 450 g

DIMENSIONS

$1/16$ inch = 2 mm
$1/8$ inch = 3 mm
$1/4$ inch = 6 mm
$1/2$ inch = 1.5 cm
$3/4$ inch = 2 cm
1 inch = 2.5 cm

OVEN TEMPERATURES

250°F = 120°C
275°F = 140°C
300°F = 150°C
325°F = 160°C
350°F = 180°C
375°F = 190°C
400°F = 200°C
425°F = 220°C
450°F = 230°C

BAKING PAN SIZES

Utensil	Size in Inches/Quarts	Metric Volume	Size in Centimeters
Baking or	$8 \times 8 \times 2$	2 L	$20 \times 20 \times 5$
Cake Pan	$9 \times 9 \times 2$	2.5 L	$23 \times 23 \times 5$
(square or	$12 \times 8 \times 2$	3 L	$30 \times 20 \times 5$
rectangular)	$13 \times 9 \times 2$	3.5 L	$33 \times 23 \times 5$
Loaf Pan	$8 \times 4 \times 3$	1.5 L	$20 \times 10 \times 7$
	$9 \times 5 \times 3$	2 L	$23 \times 13 \times 7$
Round Layer	$8 \times 1 1/2$	1.2 L	20×4
Cake Pan	$9 \times 1 1/2$	1.5 L	23×4
Pie Plate	$8 \times 1 1/4$	750 mL	20×3
	$9 \times 1 1/4$	1 L	23×3
Baking Dish	1 quart	1 L	—
or Casserole	$1 1/2$ quart	1.5 L	—
	2 quart	2 L	—